About Time

About Time

POEMS

Diane Mintz

© COPYRIGHT 2023
BY **Diane Mintz**
diane.mintz@gmail.com

All rights reserved. This book or any portion thereof may not be reproduced or used in any manner whatsoever without the express written permission of the author except for the use of brief quotations in a book review.

ISBN: 978-1-7321850-5-0

COVER DESIGN & TYPOGRAPHY:
Helene Berinsky
hb48.design@gmail.com

INTERIOR DESIGN & TYPOGRAPHY:
D. Patrick Miller • Fearless Literary
www.fearlessbooks.com

To Mark

CONTENTS

Miracles 1
That Poem 2
Urban Turkeys 4
Uncertainty 5
Loss of Words. 6
Tense 7
A Stitch in Time. 8
Feet on the Ground 10
Morning Walk 11
A Walk with God. 12
Ants 13
Pandemic Treats 14
Weeds 15
Sex 16
DNA 17
Do Habits Die?. 18
Open Book 19
Kindness 20
They Also Serve 21
Breathing 22
Deep Cleaning 24
Afternoon Dog Walk 25
Walking in the Others' Shoes 26
Broken Hallelujah. 27

Promise Me	28
Light	29
Selfless	30
Moon Shadow	31
Thinking of Yeats	32
Gone for Good	33
Survivors	34
Sportsman	35
Grandma	36
An Early Story	38
J'Accuse	39
Monday is Yellow	40
Approval	41
Blood Type	42
Daddy	44
Post-Op	45
The Junk Dealer	46
A Delicate Balance	47
The Olive Orchard	48
In the Beginning	49
Blues	50
Moving Forward	52
Blotted Out	54
Belonging	55
About Time	56

Miracles *(inspired by Albert Einstein)*

Nothing is a miracle or everything is.
Unlike relativity, this idea is graspable.

Alert and awake everything can evoke
wonder. We can be struck with awe
at the caterpillar inching toward a juicy leaf,
at the delicate tracery on the leaf, at the
caterpillar's tenacity hanging on to the leaf
swaying in the breeze, at its persistence in
pursuit of its goal, at the very existence of
this being and that it knows when and how to
wrap itself into a disguise of its own making
while it magically transforms into another miracle,
a being so unlike the earthbound caterpillar
that we would doubt its origin had we not just
watched it emerge unfolding its nascent wings.

That Poem

I want to write a poem as elegant as old lace,
as simple and airy as a child's rhyme,
as soft and loved as a stuffed animal,
as welcoming as an old slipper, as easy to slip on.

A poem in which I can open my most tender secrets
to the trusted and compassionate reader who takes in
the words knowingly, securing them inside her secret place
where she will turn to them often for solace.

Not a poem with curated advice nor old wisdom, just
an encounter, sweet and unencumbered as a baby's first
toddle down the sidewalk picking up treasures — a pebble,
the remains of a squirrel's peanut — overlooked by others.

It will not ignore what is misshapen, warped by the daily
encounters which leave bruises and blisters, not unlike
manatee skin etched with scars left by passing pleasure boats.

This poem will see both heads and tails at the same
time, welcome the reader with words of comfort while
acknowledging where hurt is still in need of healing.
It will enable new skin to grow over those wounds.

If there were such powerful medicine, a poem that can see and heal, comfort and console, I would read it day and night, give it as gifts to my loved ones and rub its magic on all who suffer.

Urban Turkeys

Traffic stops while the turkeys saunter, jaywalking across the street, spaced widely apart, their wattles swaying as they lift and place each scaly foot on the asphalt.

Yesterday drivers waited politely in a long line of cars on San Pablo Avenue while a male finished mating a female in the middle of the street. Not one driver honked.

That day I came home to find a turkey sitting on the edge of our roof. These lumbering, awkward birds can actually lift their bodies into the air when they want to.

Uncertainty

Perhaps my love of stripes and symmetry is an
expression of my need for order, my discomfort
with chaos, a desire for the simple and predictable.
A child's wish lived as an aesthetic choice.

When shopping it is a challenge to avert my
eyes from the compelling allure of stripes:
my wardrobe is evidence of my failure to
look away.

Mario Botta's entry stairway in the lobby
of the SF MOMA was my dream come true.
The entire room was in bold black and white
stripes with an elegantly centered stairway.

The clarity and simplicity of the symmetry
was like milk and cookies for me. All is
well it said. The sky is not falling and tomorrow
will arrive from the east with the sunrise.

Loss of Words

Where did sublime and resplendent go?
How about august, grand and majestic?
Have our lives become duller, flattened,
more timid? Were these words reserved
only for royalty? Did democracy deprive
us of the exalted? Or, perhaps, our move
away from the pomp of religion has made
us shy of lofty words, a little too "gloria in
excelsis deo". Not so cool. Or, sadder, what
if our lives have lost the luminousness of
grandeur? What if our aspirations are
reduced to nothing more meaningful than
money, mansions and cars? What if we have
limited ourselves to the puny and practical?
Are stars less brilliant now that we have reached
the moon and Mars?

Tense

Grammarians must have known how difficult
it would be to keep past, present, and future separated.
Past slips over the border into future without a blink.
Present has the most porous borders, slipping
easily back and forth through time.

Each moment is an exquisite island before it tumbles
unceremoniously into the future like water free-
falling from a cliff. I remind myself to savor bird
music, the sweetness of lemon blossoms, the child
chanting as she jumps rope.

Oblivious of time and safe from human interference,
cells divide, growing fat with new life, shedding dead
cells. On the ground before me insects scurry in panic
as I dig holes for new plants. I heedlessly disturb
the spiderweb anchored to a leaf.

Mostly I slip through time and space without a
foothold, unaware of these tenuous connections.
I am a mote on the earth which is dwarfed by the
ungraspable expanse of space and its unknown universes.
Would that I were able to take nothing for granted.

A Stitch in Time

Hours are stitched together
with snippets of Now and Then.

In laughter, Now overrides Then.
At other times, the two coexist

more or less peacefully until bedtime
when Then dominates the night

leaving shadowy images infused
with feelings which fade in the light.

Consciousness controls a small
space while the unconscious is

sprawled gracelessly over a vast
territory incorporating time from

the beginning, remembered or not.
I am owned by synapses firing

silently without requesting permission
or announcing presence.

I often lose my balance, slipping
over memories cowering in the

corners, long out of sight, hoping
not to be disturbed by prodding

thoughts searching among memory
scraps for lost connections.

Perhaps best to leave what is safely
hidden undisturbed by daylight

and to warm myself contentedly
in the glow of today's sun.

Feet on the Ground

Being sent in a rocket to Mars
holds no interest. In fact, I'm no
longer tempted by travel at all.
Moving closer to nothingness, I am
using the passport I got at birth to
notice the antics of the squirrels on
our walks, how they hold perfectly
still as we move forward crunching
autumn leaves under our shoes, how
the dog's nose quivers when a new
scent wafts her way, how the jasmine
reaches out to secure its hold, how if
I hold still I can feel the sound of the
hummingbird's wings, how the kid on
the corner has added a tattoo (this one
of a gorilla pounding his chest), how our
neighbor tenderly bends over her roses,
how I can still feel the childhood innocence
in my middle-aged son, how I can feel
the pain of those who speak their hearts
into an abyss, and how much I look
forward to our evenings on the couch
watching a movie with the dog curled
between us.

Morning Walk

After rain the snails with their glisten-y black bodies
and olive-drab armor are out in number.
They criss-cross footpaths at their peril.
The dog and I are walking through a field dotted with
bald white mushrooms also urged to life by the
rain. I'm keeping an eye out for my joie-de-vivre.

Today I saw an endangered Western Burrowing Owl through
the fence protecting it. It had white-tipped feathers, pupils
ringed with yellow, head swiveling on the alert.
The dog checks-in with casual glances over her shoulder.
Like the rain, the animals are a salve for heart-heaviness.

As kids we slid gleefully down the slide in the playground.
Now friends and family are silently sliding into oblivion.
Politely, they are taking turns. Your mother's turn has come.
In the morning's obits I find familiar names and cock my head
in search of the memories attached to that name lest I let
them go unacknowledged.

It is November already. Sap-less leaves crinkle underfoot
boldly announcing their last days in eye-popping color.
There's plenty yet to discover: new paths to refresh old ideas.
I do not want to linger nor to rush toward the exit.
What's not to love about the crimson treetops I see as I write.

A Walk with God

I had heard that one could meet Buddha on the road.
"Buddha is you; Buddha is me," we used to sing.
But two days ago while walking the dog I met God.
He said "hi" as we passed on the sidewalk and
then God accompanied me for the rest of the walk.
He was pleasant and tried to be conversational.
He said he had been homeless for six years. When
I asked about his health, he showed me the plastic
bracelet from his recent hospitalization. I asked
if he took his meds. "No," he explained that they
made him groggy. We chatted amiably but I could
not follow his meaning. I told him so and he
accepted that as a simple fact. He is 29 years old,
far from family, and sleeping outside in the cold
and rain. What do you need? I asked. A pillow,
he said. Are you hungry? Yes, a bit. Where do
you get food? I could not understand his answer.
I had no plan, and I trusted that God was not a
violent person so when we reached my house I
asked him to wait and I brought out a pillow with
an embroidered pillowcase, a gift from long ago.
"Do you want a sandwich," I asked. I made him
two cheese sandwiches and asked if he needed
a bag with handles to carry them. He left with the
pillow and two sandwiches in a fabric bag with handles.
The next day we found the sandwiches in the bag
in our driveway.

Ants

Life feels slow these viral days, even as it rushes on.
The hoped-for rain seeps into the welcoming earth.
Ants crawl through every crevice in the house.

The ants march with purpose and vigor finding every
point of entry no matter how we try to block their
passage. They are the stronger species.

We too marched and chanted; we read and reasoned.
What happened to our pursuit? The need didn't
disappear: we were no match for the forces against us.

The fabric of the collective us is being rent by unreason.
Cacophonous anger leaks through the cracks in the
foundation under us.

We hope that like ants whose homes are washed away
with every rain, there are enough of us to rebuild.
Childlike, I trust that ideals cannot be uprooted.

Pandemic Treats

Pandemic life has reduced my pleasures.
Spring still brings fragrant blossoms, the whir
of hummingbird wings and pollen-hungry bees
diving into the throats of patient flowers.

The dog is not alone looking forward to her treats.
I'm not nearly as adorable nor single-minded. On
these shapeless days I too reward myself with treats.
Dark chocolate for comfort.

I adjusted quickly to the new quiet and reduced
choices. Perhaps I am, like you, a secret introvert
lost in my chattering mind and the writers I turn to.
Day after quiet day. I miss maskless contact.

There is an emptiness where spice and spontaneity
used to be. Pleasant surprise used to upend the
humdrum. Now I look deeper into the ordinary and
discern a glint of what could be special if I squint just so.
.

Weeds

As a child I apologized to each weed as I pulled it out.
Now I am all business as I uproot intruders who upset
the delicate balance of color and shape I've created.

The abutilon and the red salvia blossoms open innocently
awaiting the bees and hummingbirds searching for pollen.
The flax upholds its fibrous spears in perfect balance with
the multi-headed achillea and surrounding carex grasses.

My garden is a puny antidote to the harm inflicted these
days by those who pursue power no matter the cost.
I am reminded of an old song in which a bass voice repeats
with authority "you will be mine, you will be mine all mine."

Recently, I began carrying pepper spray at night for the
last dog walk of the day at 9 p.m.
The lawlessness in the news erodes my sense of safety.
Many have no safe harbor.

Sex

Sex is a fig leaf.
Like bonobos we use sex to keep
the peace. And to make peace.
Or, if not peace, not war.
And, sex in search of love.
Bored sex. Angry sex.
Sex as a bargaining chip.
Jealous sex: "I'm the one, aren't I?"
Sex to convince yourself that this is the
right person, the right gender. Sex to
shore up insecurity. Sex to assert
dominance. Sex to submit.
Sex to cover for a secret.
Sex as a distraction. Sex is sold
with and without money.

Abstinence too is a bag of choices.
The biggest fig leaf of all.
A desire for purity. (Sex is dirty.)
To protect, protest, define, deceive,
deny, call attention to, hide behind,
to assert difference. Indifference.
It too can be a commodity.
It is declared. Declaimed. Decried.
Dolled up. Held aloft. Encouraged.
And, finally, seen for what it is:
an expression of fear. Life denying.

DNA

Once the future was so large, so expansive that I
could not count the ways: it was the soft pillow
on which I rested my sleepy head and on which
I woke to joy and possibility.

Ignorance can be its own reward, a
world free of what-could-go-wrong is,
after all, a world at peace with itself.

When I die I will not be leaving for a better
world, but just accepting the deal I didn't
know I made at birth (I should have read the fine print).

The prospect of death has its upsides: not caring
nor wanting. The world doesn't need me to
uphold its virtue: I am tired of trying and
wanting. Desire and death are the Ds in DNA.

Do Habits Die?

I do not remember beginner's mind. A tabula rasa
on which to print fresh observations free of punctuation
and excuses. I replay encounters, echoes of conversations
where I missed the point or inadvertently caused hurt.

Sometimes I feel like Lady Macbeth: Will I be
cleansed of worn-out thoughts before I die?
I still chew on old snippets like a mouse nibbling
on a telephone wire until only static remains.

But I am still new to love. I had no practice as a kid,
so it's hard to get it right. I have hit the wrong chords
so many times that I learned to live with dissonance.
Finally I know that one can learn to stay on pitch.

Doe, a deer, a female deer. Ray, a drop of golden sun.
Mi, a name, a weary me ready to unload vanity and the
need to be right for an afternoon walking down the street
holding hands while licking a mocha chip ice cream cone.

Open Book

Who is an open book anyway?
Maybe at the beginning, long
before we could read, when our thighs
and arms were creased with baby fat
and our eyes as wide as picture windows.
But there wasn't much to hide then.

From that moment when we lied about
eating the cookies we knew were for dessert,
we have known that we are capable of
duplicity. We mastered the look of
innocence early, eyes downcast with
humility, foot absently pawing the ground.

Years later the secrets are safe with me, if
only I could remember in which drawer
or closet I hid them. At the time I
crammed them in so that even I would
not know that innocence is merely a fiction.

Kindness

I envied the female crow being groomed
on the telephone line in front of my window.
At the male's tender persistence, she cocked
her head left and right offering him better
access to bury his beak in her feathers.
She accepted his ministrations as her due.
Her nonchalance as touching as his caring

They Also Serve

Milton was going blind when he wrote
"They also serve who only stand and wait."
He needed to feel forgiven for no longer
writing poems of praise. His devotion
had been the engine of his poems.

Ode to Joy, the choral work at the end of
Beethoven's triumphal 9th symphony,
was the first time a composer united
choir and orchestra. He didn't hear one
note of his work. He wrote it while deaf.

My sight and hearing are both intact.
Yet I often fail to see through my limitations
and to hear beyond what my ears detect.
I missed your despair in the noise and stridency
of our argument. I am sorry.

Breathing

I am alive, though
at times less than
fully present.

My eyes are open but
sometimes I only see
through my mind's eye.

I want to squeeze the juice
from every minute even if
I am too full to drink it all.

I allow myself long absences
from the moment, instead
remembering and reflecting

on moments of little consequence.
Perhaps writing this poem
is just that: an escape from

presence, writing with no
purpose nor hope of sending
it into the world, merely

engaging parts of myself in play,
fitting together pieces of the
puzzle that I am.

Often pieces are missing
and some of them do not
interlock properly.

Would that I could see
see the whole picture
at one time.

Deep Cleaning

I am lighter than I was and getting lighter as
I jettison the weight of what no longer matters.
Like unhealthy fat, I am shedding brittle
memories, so old that they crumble, dried
to dust from lack of usefulness.
I am deep cleaning.

Often I took myself too seriously, trying to
explain the unexplainable. The past remains
unmoved by my realizations. It is not
amenable to my need to assuage guilt or
relieve old pain. Expectations are cooked
into our food and sewn into our clothes.

These days Lewis Carroll-like characters
clamor for attention. The White Rabbit
and the Queen of Hearts parade noisily in the
public square with shrill demands. Absurdity
is not new. For now, let our remaining days
be lived quietly within the calm of shared joy.

Afternoon Dog Walk

The Marina is a sea of green; stalks of new grass extend all the
 way to the Bay.
One major rain and the earth has responded like one who was
 love-starved, now restored to robust vitality.
We cautiously hope for full reservoirs and the end to
 water-longing.

Foxy scampers over the hills whose folds are now covered
 with the new lushness.
She pokes her nose into mole tunnels with soft bumpers of
 newly excavated earth.
Formations of brown pelicans point their ample beaks
 westward toward San Francisco's formidable skyline.

Foxy leads me cross-country, away from walkways, willy nilly
 through the emerald hills.
The sun is blinding on its way to the horizon while the wind is
 bringing the beginnings of night chill.
I feel the peace of goal-less wandering while sharing
 the earth's joy.
I am in need of a tail so that I can wag my mood.

Walking in the Others' Shoes

As a Jewish child, I loved babysitting on Christmas eve
so that I could watch midnight mass on television.
The music and solemnity of the finely produced theater
filled me to tears with nameless longing, a raw yearning
to be joined with others beyond doubt or debate.

These days I am moved by the ritual of vehicles moving
aside to allow an ambulance safe passage. We are joined,
jolted out of traffic's flow, in an act of collective compassion.
At the siren's insistence we agree to delay our own arrival
so that we create a sacred space for the invisible patient.

Broken Hallelujah (*after Leonard Cohen*)

The 18th century Hasids assured their followers
that prayer doesn't require knowing the words.
Humming or even whistling will do.
Singing out of tune is also acceptable praise.

    Hallelujah

Still I try to get it right, to stay in tune, to be perfect.
I remind myself that "there is a crack in everything,"
that I am devoted to an illusion.
Habits of a lifetime trump understanding.

    Hallelujah

I envy those who have an automatic dispensation.
They have an address to appeal for forgiveness.
For me there is no deus ex machina.
My only choice is to accept my limitations.

    Hallelujah

Lila li lila li li li li li
Lila li lila li li li li li
Li li li li li li li li
Li li li li li li li Li li li li li.

    Amen

Promise Me

So much skin, you said,
in bed for the first time.
The thrill was electric.

Your smile was like a lit fuse,
a radiant sun after years
of living underground.

The intensity and intimacy
were drugs I could not refuse.
I wanted more.

Like a locust emerging after 17 years,
I finally had my wings…
what I'd always wanted.

Then my mind intruded.
It wanted assurances.
And forever.

Light

I fell in love the moment I saw him at the
center of an animated group. He was radiant.
The sun shone on his head of curls, and his smile
drew in the others. For years, I loved him while
wanting what he could not give: to cast his light
on me above all others.

His love was as light as the gauzy wing of a mayfly.
Mine was as thick as London fog.

Together we studied Talmud and karate, climbed
mountains in the snow and sun and slept under
moonlight on the top of Half Dome in Yosemite.
I was eaten by curiosity when he followed a guru in
India. I devoured books, photos, his letters, and still
remained hungry. He was unafraid to venture afield.

I marveled at his ability to reach toward the unknown.
I was jealous of the women who were drawn to his light.

He loved me as he could until our time was up.
It was as though a gong sounded sending us to
our separate corners. His radiance had been the
lure; but the constancy I needed remained elusive.
I stayed with him until I learned how to illuminate
my own path.

Selfless

She lay there barely moving.
Under her sheet a foam egg crate; on top a protector
 against accidents.
Oxygen comes through a cannula in her nostrils.
Her voice trails off into barely discernible mumbling.
We guess she cannot sustain the breath for speaking.
She smiled wanly when we entered. She did not protest
 when we left.
A mirthless giggle capped off answers to simple questions,
 a life-long habit.
She did not initiate conversation but tried to be responsive
 to our questions.
Who painted the rock on your bedside table? "My mother did,"
 she said.
She told us that she felt fine; no complaints.
In the hall a woman clutched and stroked an infant-sized doll.
The television screen in her room is black.
Maybe she no longer needs the comfort of diversions.
She surprised us with a clear response when we asked about
 her parents:
her mother was a good mother; her father was not a good
 father, nor husband.
The past is still peopled; the present is flat, uninflected.
She is dying with fragments of self.

Moon Shadow

On our last walk at 9 pm, Foxy and I are accompanied by the moon shape-shifting through its phases. I'm grateful for its benign constancy despite the earth's precarity.

At the same time, I am angry at those who presume the moon to be theirs to conquer, a new thing on which they can carve their names like school kids on their desktops.

The moon's luminous presence was not affected by the planting of national flags on its surface, pitiable proof of the petty competition to be the first.

Each of us — and our planet — is still an elegant egg in the sweet hum of creation. Flags are not enough to obscure the enormity of all we do not and will never know.

Thinking of Yeats

Centrifugal force of habit keeps us glued to the walls
as they spin. "The center will not hold."
We are heedless of the signs.

Our nightmare: a truck is on fire, barreling toward
us, but we're unable to move out of the way.
Fires scorch our waking reality; there is no water.

The air is thick with particulates.
Breathing is harmful.
Animals cannot find a safe place.

We are living in an old Hollywood western:
the bad guy is shooting at our feet.
We have no choice but to keep dancing.

Gone for Good

On that day, the day that the last white rhino died,
we didn't stop in our tracks to say goodbye nor allow grief
to overtake us. We kept moving toward our own last day.

He left no descendants. The road ended sharply.
We did not take notice. The Buddhists say that every
blade of grass has equal importance. Each being belongs.

He and his kind have vanished for good. There is now
a hole in the universe where they belonged.
Remembering cannot restore us to wholeness.

I fear for all of us, the bees who perish in the heat,
the polar bears who have lost their very ground,
and we who cling to denial as our means of survival.

Survivors

The monarch butterfly, on the verge of extinction,
doesn't know that this season its eggs might not
survive to complete their cycle.
Undeterred, the monarch is obedient
to its nature, perfectly in tune.
Joy wells up at each monarch sighting.
We root for the return to the natural order
in which we too have a place.

As a child I wondered how Holocaust survivors
could ever smile again. Today I read of a 99-
year old survivor who, when she died, was the
lead person in a heavy metal band. It pleased
her, maybe even gave her joy, to venture into
new realms, to open her wings to the world just
like an emerging monarch.

Sportsman

On 60 Minutes last night I watched as a
hunter with a high-powered rifle took aim
at a grazing bison whose only movement
was his jaws munching the grass at his feet.
Even a small child could hit a bison broadside.

Grandma

She kept strictly kosher, even a separate bar of
soap for milk and meat. My father loved her
sabbath cholent, on the stove and ready from
sundown on Friday until three stars on Saturday.
He ate her cholent with evident pleasure while
holding an old grudge.

On our weekend visits, she spoke Yiddish to my father.
On Rosh Hashanah we walked to shul and back for her
holiday meal. Though a widow, she was a real balabusta,
the accomplished mistress of her home. I remember those
visits: relatives spoke accented English punctuated with
Yiddish.

She worked for a furrier and wore a Persian lamb coat.
She had crimson lipstick and manicured nails. One of
seven from shtetl poverty in the Old Country, in
America she dressed the part of a woman of means.
After her husband died she married a quiet man who
peddled in the streets of Newark with his horse and cart.

When I was seven or eight, a few days before Christmas — a
day we did not celebrate — grandma came over bearing gifts.
My mother had gone to the cellar to stoke the furnace;

the apartment was toasty as we opened the presents. She had brought us stockings for Santa which we hung on the wall over our nonexistent fireplace.

I never learned what frayed the thread between mother and son.
In leaving the East Coast and the warmth of traditional ways, he leaped bravely into a new, unfamiliar world where he never got a foothold. Always teetering, he had made his choice and remained adamant through gritted teeth.

Her weekly letters always began "How are you? Fine I hope."

An Early Story

The time I smeared feces into the grooves
of the crib slats with joy and abandon
I was too young to clean up the mess,
also too young to apologize.
I was free as a baby.

What if I had slithered under the tsk-tsking
which surely followed and wrapped myself
in that abandon? There might have been more
knee scrapes, some broken bones, but less
fear of speeding downhill.

Most of us do not tell our early stories
or keep track of exuberances not
captured in the classic milestone photos.
Hopes and regrets die with the dead, even
of those who cleaned up my mess.

Stories hang suspended in the air like atoms
waiting to jump on the right molecule to
bring their messages to life. At the time,
I didn't know which self I wanted to preserve
for posterity.

J'Accuse

Every Friday Sara cleaned our apartment.
The smell of simmering chicken soup filled the kitchen.
(At dinner my broth was dotted with tiny chicken eggs.)
Sara ironed while the soup simmered on the stove.
The soup's aroma mixed with the steam of the damp cloth.

My lie that day has squirmed in me like a worm on a hook.
I was seven and a bit of a drama queen. Was my story
made up on the spot, testing my power to move an
audience? Once spoken it was too late to wonder.

Suddenly I was one of the insiders and Sara was an
outsider accused by a child in her employers' home.
That long-ago guile crystalized into guilt, a painful
memory for me but loss and hardship for Sara.

How did I know that Sara was powerless?

Monday is Yellow

Monday is yellow we agreed, lying side by side on our
identical twin beds. Monday was bright and welcoming.
Tuesday was darker. Deep blue, leaning toward black
   in low light.

After agreeing on the color of each day, we would take
turns reaching our arms to the other's bed so that we could
tickle, rub, scratch lightly on the soft skin of the other's forearm
   until sleep separated us.

I left you behind early, never seeing your outstretched arms.
You were the nice one, the good one; I didn't know you
   needed me.
At the end I took care of you the way you always wanted:
   big sister caring.
You died in my arms. I didn't know that knots tied early
   cannot be untied.

Approval

"It's a shame your father never loved you,"
my demented mother said.
Out of the mouths of babes.

For years I girded myself with armor,
closing off chambers of my heart
in pursuit of a dead man's acceptance.

Stretching awake to spring, sniffing the air,
I am surprised at the absence of danger.
Touch me. I no longer bite.

Blood Type

She began early hiding from the world.
High school was out of the question.
Her father lied to the truant officer.
Her blood type was F for fear.

She married young and her fear
lurked between them like a shadow.
"Mama mama," I heard her crying when I was three.
I went to their room to console her.

Later when she sang at our bedside, she told us about
the kitten she had once found and hidden in a drawer,
of swimming and roller skating with neighborhood kids.
I mixed the joy in her stories into the batter of childhood,
    hers and mine.

Her great pleasure was dressing up on Saturdays for their
    night out.
From the sensual crystal bottles on her dresser she dabbed
    behind her ears.
Then she leaned over the sink closer to the mirror to apply
    blood-red lipstick.
Over time she shaped the lipstick still in the tube into a
    sharp angle.

I still have to cover my ears remembering her screams
    as we drove up
the steep curvy road on a day trip to the observatory.
Her pleas to pull over went unheeded.
We thought he was the problem.

He died at 67. I did not cry.
She cried until she moved to a community
where she dressed in poofy petticoats
square dancing with utter delight.

Without him she bounced between depression
and clap-your-hands glee
until dementia swallowed her whole.
"Are you watching me die?" she asked as I tucked her in.

Daddy

You made me a fighter.
I would not be humbled,
constrained, limited,
commanded by your
arbitrary authority.
Like a rodent I
burrowed under rules
with subterfuge and lies.
I graduated to calculated
rebellion. Your no became
my automatic yes. Too stubborn
to show pain, I refused to cry.
Girls can and I did; I did not have
a plan; I did not know where I was
going, but I went. I did not stop
to know what I felt; I did not know
where to look for peace. Long
after you died, I continued running
just to stay ahead of you. Only
now that I have outpaced my
pursuer by years can I stop
to catch my breath.
Now I have the time to
acknowledge your pain.

Post-Op

When the orderly wheeled you from surgery
into recovery, we three sat waiting for news.
Mom stood ready to go in to see you when —
imagine our surprise — he said that you
asked for me. Me. Me your adversary.

You were a jumble of tubing coming
from your head, arms and chest,
still groggy from the anesthetic.
With reluctance I took the hand closest
to me and held it gently. You and I
had not been hand-holders.

We remained mostly silent. I began
to move my thumb over the top of
your hand as in a caress. Now, years
later, I can only think that we had
leaped beyond the need to apologize.

The Junk Dealer

It was hard work lifting barrels of scrap metal.
Copper, nickel, steel, shards, wires, and plates.
He was proud of having learned the names of
all the metals on his truck.

He was always his own boss, but he scraped and
pleased like an employee. End of year schnapps for this
customer, babka for another, an apology for that one.
The barrels were heavy, but it was a living.

Before this he had delivered bread at 4 a.m., meats
(hot dogs, bologna, and other cold cuts), seltzer,
kosher pickles, greeting cards, lingerie, insurance.
It was never a living.

The son of immigrants, he didn't go to high school.
His shame became a mantra for his children: they
would go to college so that they could have a better life.
A better living.

A Delicate Balance

Where are you going? she would ask
every time we approached the door.
Old photos showed a pretty young
woman. Fear not visible.

Her thoughts slid out of her mouth
like speech bubbles in a comic book.
On that day that she read my letters
to a friend, silence filled the house.

When she finally spoke, she spit out
the worst names she could think of.
I had gone out the good girl door
but veered off the narrow path.

Her image of me was ripped up like an
old photo. Glue could not make it whole.
Her world was now off its axis, and a
15-year-old was left to restore balance.

The Olive Orchard

I was assigned olive picking.
The boss was a square-jawed, curly-haired man
who spoke no English.
My Hebrew was new and halting.
We pickers climbed ladders with a rigid-bottomed
sack draped over our necks. We chose a branch,
placed it over the sack's opening, and ran our
fingers down the branch.
The olives dropped into the mouth of the sack.
Pleasant work.
The boss gave us directions and then said little else.
Shy, I thought. I was on an adventure; he was attractive.
He and his buddies said I looked like Julie Andrews.
They had had a bet whose bed I would wind up in.

In the Beginning

I was beautiful then.
Skin taut over an enormous belly,
blue veins sketched from the inside.

I loved you fiercely even before you
emerged. I saw you through eyes
that found you flawless.

The miracle was that you came
from my body. I was prose;
you were poetry.

You latched on and nourishment
flowed to fill you as my joy too
was overflowing.

My only job was to love you,
like sap flowing to the tree roots.
You blossomed in season.

You were magnetic, magical.
He was immediately superfluous.
You were essence, essential.

Blues

How did blue come to mean sadness?
I am down and blue. When my baby done left
me the blues were waiting for me. To have
the blues is to suffer. It is cursed among colors,
with the possible exception of cowardly yellow.
But now that there aren't so many old-school
cowboy movies, cowardice seems to have been
left to wither. The Cowardly Lion on the Yellow
Brick Road to Oz was actually quite lovable.

Blues persist. In the old days of Robert Johnson
and Leadbelly, blues were the authentic expression
of insurmountable poverty and more than their share
of violence. Well-heeled singers have adopted the
style, if not the circumstances of its origins.
Many have even been accepted into the pantheon,
though it is jarring to hear blues played by those
who assume the style in the absence of dead-end lives.

Purity, like perfection, is just a word with no roots in real
life. Imitation is a sly word which intends to shame those
inspired by others. But we all take from those who came
first. Bob Dylan grabbed the zeitgeist of the 60's with his
blues styling. Miles Davis had his own kind of blue. And,
in her album, Blue, Joni Mitchell invents a new idiom in

which to sing her angst. They, and others, changed the blues to suit their time. They mixed the old with something new, but the new is still painted blue.

Moving Forward

Though slight, I have substance.
Not weighty, though not airy.
Yet in the past I allowed myself to
be blown about, on to the next
thing, the next event, the next
lover, moving forward without a
plan or direction, just forward,
moving because I wasn't able to
to stay still. Maybe the next thing
might bring something coated in
sweetness, the next encounter a
a new flavor, a new way of seeing,
of being, of creating a space which
might open to unforeseeable wonder.

Now, forward is a fraught direction.
It still can be new and have a tinge
of mystery, but now I can guess what
might be behind the door, in the box,
just barely discernible in the distance.
In writing I have found purchase in
this place, this time, this line, this
mind. In writing I can combine times,
change my mind, tell the truth
without tearing a hole in the fabric

of my peace. I can sit still, focus
backward and forward, in and out,
and still hold on to my substance.

Blotted Out

Though old, I am grateful that
my mind has not yet been
blotted out, memories bleeding
into each other like ink smeared
across a page, stealing sense and
meaning from time's vault,
mushing together first and last,
blame and fault, leaving only
a few scribbles hanging on to
the bottom of the page.
Afflicted souls often recall mother,
the love imprinted into every
nerve fiber giving self a space
and a name to live with.
Now, with fear for the vanishing self,
these souls lose footing and fall
into the vast abyss of time and space.
In the blur, brows knit with confusion
as they return to nothingness.
The lost trudge through a
landscape devoid of the living,
a ghoulish parade of those long gone.

Belonging

Yesterday I turned 80, still as unthinkable
as borrowing a stranger's underwear or
getting lost in another country where the
words make no sense. I could have sworn
I didn't get on that plane: I am still here
where, until yesterday, the future was vast.

But, I do belong right here. I have traveled
all the days and time zones it took to arrive
to this place. I belong to all the life around me,
growing and dying before my eyes. The fragile
blossom borne of the succulent at my backdoor,
the one which lived for only 24 hours is my sister.

I belong because I am alive and moving toward
my own demise. I am a creature not separate
from the squirrels in our yard and the jasmine
covering the trellis. With them I share the
earth and the air we breathe. Without them
I would be bereft.

About Time

There are so few eggs left in my basket
that I can clearly see the bottom.
When the basket was full I didn't care
how many were lost or broken. Now
scarcity makes each one precious.

I smile to myself mornings while stretching
and doing my jumping jacks accompanied
by a bouncy soundtrack. All an effort to
keep me from becoming like the Tinman
on the road to Oz.

When I lose myself to the pleasure of
a good movie as I lick my evening
fudgsicle or pet the dog just to
revel in her joy, tomorrow is purely
hypothetical; now fills me up.

Winter's chill has kept me from my dear
garden. The neglect is obvious: the ground
is dense with dead leaves and weeds.
I am impatient for spring and the soothing
warmth for my reunion with each plant.

Joy, like a baby's giggle, floats free of
concerns not of this moment, a respite
from predictions of future disaster.
May joy and kindness prevail, even if it
happens long after my basket is empty.

www.ingramcontent.com/pod-product-compliance
Lightning Source LLC
Chambersburg PA
CBHW060412080526
44583CB00012B/541